hot dogs
and
dinosnores

Amanda Li is a children's writer who likes jokes. And animals. Which is why she's written this very funny animal joke book.

Knock, knock . . .
Who's there?
Jane.
Jane who?
Jane who did the drawings in this book.

(That's **Jane Eccles**, who loves drawing and works in a tiny room in her house in Hampshire, where she lives with her husband and son and small grey cat.)

Also from Macmillan Children's Books

Jellyphants and Woolly Jumpers:
My First Joke Book
Amanda Li

Christmas Jokes

The Bumper Book of Very Silly Jokes

hot dogs
and
dinosnores

my first animal joke book

Compiled by

Amanda Li

Illustrated by Jane Eccles

MACMILLAN CHILDREN'S BOOKS

First published 2014 by Macmillan Children's Books
a division of Macmillan Publishers Limited
20 New Wharf Road, London N1 9RR
Basingstoke and Oxford
Associated companies throughout the world
www.panmacmillan.com

ISBN 978-1-4472-5373-0

3 5 7 9 8 6 4

A CIP catalogue record for this book is available from
the British Library.

Printed and bound by CPI Group (UK) Ltd, Croydon CR0 4YY

For Andy Yates - the biggest joker of all
(AL)

To my mum & dad, Zita and David Eccles
(JE)

What should you do if a dog
eats your pencil?

Use a pen instead.

What's the only kind of
dog you can eat?

A hot dog.

What do dogs eat at the cinema?

Pup-corn.

What do you call a dog who
likes bubble baths?

A sham-poodle.

Why did the dog say, 'Miaow'?

He wanted to learn a new language.

What's the difference between a dog and a flea?

A dog can have fleas – but a flea can't have a dog.

Why do dogs run in circles?

Because they can't run in squares.

**What was on special offer
at the pet shop?**

'Buy one dog, get one flea.'

Why do dogs bury bones
in the ground?

Because they can't bury
them in trees.

When is it unlucky to see a black cat?

When you're a mouse.

Why do cats make terrible
storytellers?

They only have one tail.

What did the cat say on
the racetrack?

'Miiaaooooooooooooowwwwwwww!'

What's a cat's favourite colour?

Purr-ple.

What do cats like to eat

when it's hot?

Mice cream.

Where did the kittens go for
their school trip?

To the mew-seum.

What kind of gum do bees chew?

Bumble-gum.

Why do bees hum?
Because they always
forget the words.

What did the bee say to the flower?

'Hello, honey!'

What's the biggest ant in the world?

An elephant.

What's the biggest moth
in the world?

A mammoth.

What's even smaller than
an ant's lunch?

An ant's mouth.

What do you call an ant
with ten eyes?

Ant-ten-eye!

What do you do with a sick insect?

Call an ant-bulance.

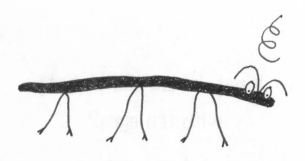

Why is the letter 't' so
important to a stick insect?

Without it. it would be a *sick* insect.

Why was the ant confused?

Because all his uncles were 'ants'.

What do you call a fly with

no wings?

A walk.

Where do spiders play football?

At Web-ley Stadium.

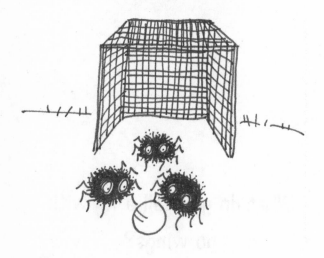

How do fireflies start a race?

'Ready, steady, glow!'

What did one flea say to the other?

'I love you aw-flea!'

What has wheels and flies?

A rubbish truck.

What kind of parties do grasshoppers go to?

Cricket balls.

What's worse than finding a slug in your sandwich?

Finding half a slug.

Why is a snail the strongest animal?

Because it carries its house
around on its back.

How do snails get ready
for a party?

They put on snail varnish.

Where can you find giant snails?

At the end of giants' fingers.

How can you tell which end
of a worm is which?

Tickle it in the middle and see
which end laughs.

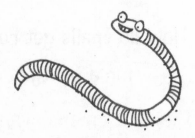

What did the early worm say
to the late worm?

'Where in earth have you been?'

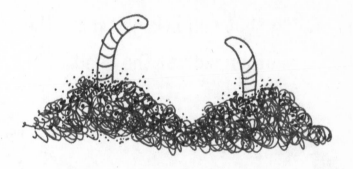

Where do caterpillars lay
their heads at night?

On their cater-pillows.

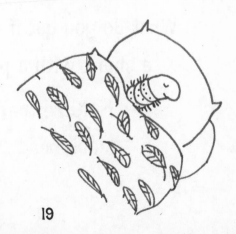

What do you get if you cross
a dog with a frog?

A dog that can lick you from the
other side of the road.

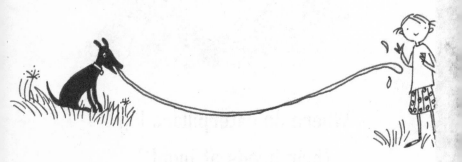

What do you get if you cross
a shark with a parrot?

A creature that talks
your head off.

What do you get when you cross
an elephant with a kangaroo?

Great big holes all over Australia.

What do you get if you cross
a parrot and a cat?

A carrot.

What do you get if you cross
a pie and a rat?

A pirate.

What do you get if
you cross a jellyfish
with a helicopter?

A jelly-copter.

What do you get if you cross a
kangaroo with a dog?

A pooch with a pouch.

What do you get if you cross
a skunk with a bat?

A nasty smell that hangs
around all day.

What do you get if you cross a
crocodile with a flower?

I don't know, but I won't
be smelling it.

What do you get if you cross
a snake and a pie?

A pie-thon.

What do you get if you cross a
cat with an elephant?

A flat cat.

What do you get if you cross a
snake with a secret agent?

A spy-thon.

What do you get if you cross
a fly, a car and a dog?

A flying carpet.

What is the biggest kind of
mouse in the world?

A hippopota-mouse.

Why did the mouse have a bath?

To get squeaky clean.

What do mice do at weekends?

Mouse-work.

Which day of the week do fish hate?

Fry-day.

What is the strongest
creature in the sea?

The mussel.

How does a shark say
hello to a fish?

'Pleased to eat you.'

Which fish sits on a plate
and wobbles?

A jellyfish.

How do whales carry big things?

In a whale-barrow.

What does a shellfish do
on its birthday?

Shell-abrate.

What's the best way to catch a fish?

Ask someone to throw it at you.

What's the worst thing
about being an octopus?

Washing your hands before dinner.

What does a jelly fish have
on its tummy?

A jelly button.

Why did the fish blush?

Because it saw the ship's bottom.

How do you make a goldfish old?

Take away the 'g'.

How did the owls get into
Noah's ark?

Two-hoo by two-hoo.

Why do hens lay eggs?
Because if they dropped
them, they'd break.

Which pies can fly?

Magpies.

Which bird is always out of breath?

A puffin.

What do ducks pull at Christmas?

Christmas quackers.

Which bird can lift the
heaviest weights?

The crane.

What time does a
duck wake up?

At the quack of dawn.

How does a duck
learn new words?

It uses a duck-tionary.

What's a cow's favourite dinner?

Moo-dles.

Why do cows wear bells?

Because their horns don't work.

How do you count a herd of cows?

With a cow-culator.

23, 24, 25, 26...

What goes 'OOOOO'!

A cow with no lips.

What do you call a cow
on a trampoline?

A milkshake.

What do cows read?

Moos-papers.

How do you get lots of
pigs on a farm?

Build a sty-scraper.

Why did the cow cross the road?

To get to the udder side.

What do you sing to a
cow on its birthday?

'Happy Birthday to Moo . . .'

How do you move a
really heavy pig?

Use a pork-lift truck.

Where do sheep get their hair cut?

At the baa-baa shop.

What do you call a sheep
with no legs?

A cloud.

What is the difference between
a horse and a duck?

One goes quick and the
other goes quack.

What do you call a sleeping bull?

A bulldozer.

How do you find out how
much a sheep costs?

Just scan the baa-code.

What do you call a pig
that does karate?

A pork chop.

There were two sheep in a field.
The first sheep turned to the
other and said, 'Baa!'

'I was going to say that!'
replied the second sheep.

Which animal goes to sleep
with its shoes on?

A horse.

What's a frog's favourite sweet?

A lolli-hop.

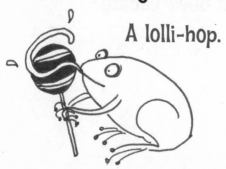

What's green and spotty?

A frog with chickenpox.

Where do sick frogs go?

To the hop-spital.

How do frogs cheer?

'Hop hop hooray!'

What do you call a seat for a toad?

A toadstool.

How do you know if a
frog has ears?

Shout, 'Free flies!' and
see if he hops over.

What kind of lion never roars?

A dandelion.

Why won't leopards play
hide-and-seek?

Because they are always spotted.

What's invisible and smells
like bananas?

A monkey's fart.

What do you call an
exploding monkey?

A ba-boom!

What do you call an untidy hippo?

A hippopota-mess.

Which animal is always laughing?

A happy-potamus.

Why is an elephant
like a tree?

They both have trunks.

Why do giraffes have
such long necks?

Because they've got
really stinky feet.

How do you know if there's an
elephant hiding under your bed?

Your nose is touching the ceiling.

What do you call an
elephant in a Mini?

Stuck.

Why don't elephants use computers?

They're afraid of the mouse.

How do elephants talk to each other?

On the ele-phone.

What do you call someone with
an elephant on his head?

Squashed.

Why do elephants live in the jungle?

Because they can't fit into a house.

What should you do if you find an
elephant in your bed?

Sleep on the sofa.

Knock, knock.

Who's there?

Hippo.

Hippo who?

Hippo birthday to you!

What's the difference between
an elephant and a postbox?

I don't know.

I won't be asking you to
post my letter then.

Knock, knock.

Who's there?

Cows go.

Cows go who?

Cows go 'Moo', silly!

Knock, knock.

Who's there?

Rabbit.

Rabbit who?

Rabbit up carefully,
it's a gift.

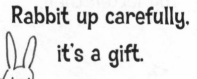

Knock, knock.

Who's there?

Gorilla.

Gorilla who?

Gorilla me a hamburger, please.

Knock, knock.

Who's there?

Barbara.

Barbara who?

Barbara black sheep,
have you any wool?

Knock, knock.

Who's there?

Owl.

Owl who?

Owl be very sad if
you don't let me in.

Knock, knock.

Who's there?

A herd.

A herd who?

A herd you were coming,
so I baked a cake.

What do you call a sleeping dinosaur?

A dino-snore.

What did dinosaurs have that
no other animals have?

Baby dinosaurs.

Which dinosaur is the scariest?

The terror-dactyl.

What do you get when a
dinosaur sneezes?

Out of the way.

What's as big as a dinosaur but
doesn't weigh anything?

A dinosaur's shadow.

What did the triceratops
wear on its legs?

Tricera-bottoms.

What do you call a penguin
in the desert?

Lost.

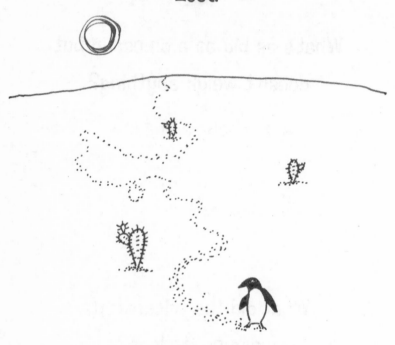

What is black and white,
black and white, black and white?

A penguin rolling down a hill.

Why do penguins carry
fish in their beaks?

Because they don't have any pockets.

Where do penguins
go to dance?

To a snowball.

What do you call a rabbit
that tells jokes?

A funny bunny.

What do you call a rabbit
with no clothes on?

A bare hare.

What did the rabbit
say to the carrot?

'It's been nice gnawing you.'

How do you catch a rabbit?

Hide behind a tree and
act like a carrot.

What are rabbits'
favourite stories?

Ones with hoppy endings.

How does the Easter bunny keep fit?

Lots of eggs-ercise.

What has twelve legs, six eyes,
three tails and can't see a thing?

The Three Blind Mice.

Where do mice park their boats?

At the hickory dickory dock.

What did the hedgehog
say to the cactus?

'Is that you, Mummy?'

What sound do hedgehogs
make when they kiss?

'Ouch!'

How do you stop a skunk
from smelling?

Hold its nose.

What do you call a camel
with three humps?

Humphrey.

What do you call a
deer with no eyes?

No eye-deer.

How do squirrels send emails?

On the Inter-nut.

What do snakes do after they've
had an argument?

Hiss and make up.

Which snakes are
good at sums?

Adders.

Which hand would you use to pick up a dangerous snake?

Someone else's.

What kind of tiles can't you stick on walls?

Reptiles.

Why do hamsters like
spinning on wheels?

Because it's wheely fun.

Why do dragons sleep all day?

So they can fight knights.

Which pet just lies around
on the floor all day?

A carpet.